This self-guided journal is not intended to treat any mental health disorder. This journal is meant to help guide you to the start of your new journey or to be used in conjunction with attending counseling or therapy to better support your goals.

Believing in yourself can be hard at times,
but it is truly amazing when you can
recognize all your capabilities.
-Jordan D. Samuelson

Table of Contents

Chapter 1: Being raw

Chapter 2: Finding your voice

Chapter 3: Staying true to yourself

Chapter 4: Finding your belief systems

Chapter 5: Gaining self-awareness for change

Chapter 6: Finding balance & self-care

Chapter 7: Boundaries

Chapter 8: Letter to new & improved self

Healing is the most powerful & wonderful

thing you can do for yourself.

-Jordan D. Samuelson

Chapter 1: Being Raw

Telling your Story

Being raw and telling your story can be: scary, anxiety provoking, sad, and at times joyful. This is a time for you to finally feel safe sharing your story, (maybe for the first time) in writing. From personal experience, once your story is written and you are able to share it out loud. After several times it loses its emotional intensity. This is especially true when it comes to dark times in our lives. So, maybe by the end of this journal, you will have found your voice or taken back control. On the pages below you will see prompts to help you start your story. The hardest part is starting, but once you do...you may surprise yourself... Feel free to write in first or third person.

Prompt ideas

- *Growing up I thought my childhood was _____*

- *When I was _ years-old I remember _____*

- *My first memory of _____*

- *One thing that was always instilled in me by _____(person) was _____ (Ex: it's not okay to show emotion)*

_____

_____

_____

_____

_____

_____

_____

_____

_____

_____

_____

_____

_____

_____

_____

_____

_____

_____

_____

Developing a growth mindset teaches

us how to evolve from failures & overcome.

-Jordan D. Samuelson

Chapter 2: Finding your voice

Implementing postive self-talk

Believe it or not, creating positive self-statements and speaking them inwardly or outwardly toward self can feel awkward and foreign. The key is practicing daily self-talk until your postive self-statements start to become second nature. Implementation of self-statements can help you learn to motivate yourself in all areas of life such as: getting out of bed, cleaning your room, going to work, and even asking your crush out on a date. Postive self-statements allow you to gain self-awareness of thoughts, feelings/emotions, and can help you rationalize and problem solve through situations and personal struggles.

Examples of postive self-talk in first person

- *I can do this*
- *Today I am grateful to be alive*
- *I do not have to let my anxiety consume me today*
- *I am strong*
- *I am enough*
- *This too shall pass and I will come out stronger because of it*
- *I can only control what I can*
- *I am deserving of love, respect, and loyalty*
- *I am honest, caring, and a supportive friend*
- *It's okay to feel how I am feeling and still take care of myself today*
- *I know this shit, and I got this shit!*

Examples of postive self-talk in third person (my personal favorite)

*Tip: sarcasm is acceptable as long as not self-degrading

- *(insert name) what are you going to do to make today a better day?*
- *(insert name) today is going to be a great day, because you are a rock star!*
- *(insert name) you can do this!*
- *(insert name) you are worthy of love*
- *(insert name) you got this!*
- *(insert name) focus on what is in your control versus out of your control*
- *(insert name) you are beautiful just the way you are!*
- *(insert name) this will pass and you will overcome this challenge*
- *(insert name) it's okay not to be okay and expand your knowledge and comfort zones to becoming a better you!*
- *(insert name) working on yourself is the greatest achievement you can do for yourself!*

My positive self-statements

1.

2.

3.

4.

5.

6.

7.

8.

9.

10.

Change your lenses from time to time

in order to gain new perspectives.

-Jordan D. Samuelson

Chapter 3: Staying true to yourself

<u>Identifying your values and beliefs</u>

Values and beliefs are characteristics that you identify with. They help define you and contribute to your decision making. Knowing your values and beliefs allows you to connect with people who align with you best. For example: if family is one of my strongest values that I believe in, then I want a partner in life that also values family. Values impact the choices we make daily and throughout our lives. Understanding our values and beliefs allow us to prioritize what matters to us and who we want to align with in our lives.

Check off the values that you align with currently (√) or would like to instill (X) into your life moving forward. This is not a comprehensive list so feel free to add your own.

____ Love		____ Adventure
____ Family		____ Goal Oriented
____ Health		____ Creativity
____ Friendship		____ Tranquility
____ Career		____ Morals
____ Wealth		____ Intelligence
____ Personal Time		____ Nature
____ Freedom		____ Beauty
____ Responsibility		____ Respect
____ Safety		____ Assertive
____ Loyalty		____ Power
____ Honesty		____ Empathy
____ Religion/Spirituality		____ Sympathy
____ Stability		____ Balance
____ Wisdom		____ Awareness
____ Independence		____ Accountabilty
____ Humor		____ Strength
____ Success		____ Integrity

Fear can be scary, but what is scarier

than fear is being stuck and not living.

-Jordan D. Samuelson

Chapter 4: Finding your belief systems

We all have automatic and/or negative patterns of thinking that have been instilled in us without realizing it-typically stemming from our childhood, but not always. Once we find out what are negative belief system is, we are able to identify each time, in our life, that this belief system was reiterated. For example, if my negative core belief is, I'm a failure, my time line thus far in my life would consist of times in my life I felt I failed myself or others.

Once we can identify our negative belief system, then we can work on changing that mindset to a postive statement or belief that we want to instill within ourself. For instance, if my belief is "I'm a failure," my new belief or postive statement might be "I am succeeding or I am doing the best I can at this point in time."

It can be at times more effective to process through your negative belief systems and moments in your life through EMDR (eye movement desensitization and reprocessing). There are many EMDR therapists trained in this field that you can find based on a simple search using a website called psychologytoday.com, or if you are already in therapy, maybe your therapist can help.

Examples of negative belief systems

Examples of postive belief systems

__ I'm not good enough

__ I'm a disappointment

__I'm a failure or I will fail

__ I have to be in control all the time

__ It's not safe to show emotions

__ I should have done something

__ I'm unlovable or I don't deserve love

__ I don't deserve…

Other negative beliefs could be regarding people, places, or things:

__People are evil

__Everyone is trying to take advantage of me

__The world is unsafe

__All men/women cannot be trusted

__Bad things happen to good people

__ I am okay just the way I am

__ I am succeeding or I am successful

__ I deserve to…

__ I can learn to…

__ I am learning to let go of…

__ I can identify what is in my control

__ I can accept my emotions and it is okay to feel and show them

__ I am worthy or love

__ I can keep myself safe or I can protect myself

__ I am good enough

__ I can see the world in my perspective

__ I can keep my safe in this world

__ I can learn to trust that others are worthy of my time

Expanding your comfort zone is learning to thrive to your new potential in life, love, career, &/or interpersonal relationships.

-Jordan D. Samuelson

Chapter 5: Gaining self-awareness for change

In order for change to occur one must be self-aware of the way they act, think, and behave. Also, the abilty to filter thoughts and emotions. When we emotionally react to something, most of the time we make a problem or situation bigger than it needs to be. On the other hand, we might be second guessing ourselves or feeling guilty…. Questioning "why did I do or say that?!" Everyone has the abilty to learn how to gain self-awareness as this does not come easy for most of us.

The first start to gaining self-awareness is to use reflection. By this I mean reflecting at the end of the day how you were feeling or thinking and where you could have made changes. I prefer to do this in a journal format. By reflecting on my day, this allows me to get everything out of my head onto paper and see the cause and effect of my thoughts and feelings. From there I am able to start gaining awareness of when I need to remove myself from certain situations, filter my thoughts to be more rational, as well as focus on when and where I need to keep my feelings in check.

On this page I want you to use it however, you please, whether it's journaling about your day, or writing down your normal thoughts, and feelings, and cause and effect of those. Below is a template to use if you would like. Remember using your own methods that work for you is okay as well (Ex. Word document, tablet, journal, dry erase board).

Thoughts	Feelings	Action	Outcome
I'm not good enough at ____	Sad, ashamed, disappointed	Quitting, giving up, shutting down	Didn't complete ____ or got into trouble.

The act of taking care of yourself

is sexy & you deserve it!

-Jordan D. Samuelson

Chapter 6: Finding balance & self-care

Let's be honest, finding balance in all areas of life is hard. As cliché as it may sound having structure and routine in your day to day life helps with stabilty, consistency, and finding balance. The hardest thing to do is to make ourselves a priority, but once you decide it's okay to be little selfish here and there, then you won't take your time for yourself for granted.

Self-care can include a variety of things such as: taking a bubble bath, lighting candles and watching your favorite movie or television show, calling a friend, spending time with a relative, going for a drive by yourself, making your favorite meal, and getting extra rest. The list goes on and on. You deserve to make yourself a priority and take care of yourself. If you don't take care of yourself, how can you be expected to be there for others?

Create a list of self-care techniques you want to implement in your daily life. This can include daily self-care, weekly, and maybe something special every month for yourself. Feel free to create your own way of planning your self-care whether in a planner, notebook, calendar, daily to-do list, or sticky notes...

My self-care plan/techniques

*

*

*

*

*

*

*

*

*

*

Setting boundaries with self and others

is the abilty to give and gain respect.

-Jordan D. Samuelson

Chapter 7: Boundaries

Setting boundaries are not only for others, but to protect and respect ourselves. Setting boundaries feels uncomfortable and out of most our comfort zones, until we build confidence in our voice and say what we mean and feel. Keep in mind boundaries should be assertive, not passive or aggressive. Therefore, be mindful of your voice and body language when setting boundaries. It is preferred to do them in person if possible so there is no room for interpretation.

You can set a boundary for just about anything whether physical or emotional. Boundaries can be loose, but also firm depending on the person you set the boundary with. For example, if someone doesn't respect your choices and thinks they always have to be right or in control, then it is almost impossible to set a loose boundary, as it is easy to break and not be taken seriously.

FYI-sometimes setting boundaries feels like your talking to a three-year-old over and over again about the same thing until some day it just clicks for them. This is what boundaries feels like for certain people in our life, whether family, friends, significant others, and coworkers. The more we reiterate our boundaries the more they will stick and we will be able to give and gain the respect we deserve. Also, saying no to someone/something we don't want to do or cannot do is also boundary setting and there is no need to justify our reasoning for saying "no."

Let's practice setting boundaries. I have included some of my personal boundaries that I still use to this day. Feel free to add your own boundaries or boundaries you would like to/need to set with people or yourself in your life.

Examples:

Please do not interrupt me while I am talking.

I am needing time to myself to take care of myself right now (you can make this time specific or more so at the end of a school or work day).

Could you please not say the word _____ around me as it makes me feel uncomfortable.

...No I am not available tonight (this weekend).

Life is about continuing the path I choose

for my life, regardless of life's trials &
tribulations.

-Jordan D. Samuelson

Chapter 8: Letter to new & improved self

The hope is that with this self-help guide you are able to see your potential new self emerge as you continue to grow. I want you to write a letter to yourself, to the new and improved you, on the pages provided or on your own paper. Remember: life has its highs and lows, but that doesn't mean the journey stops. You always have a choice to implement change!

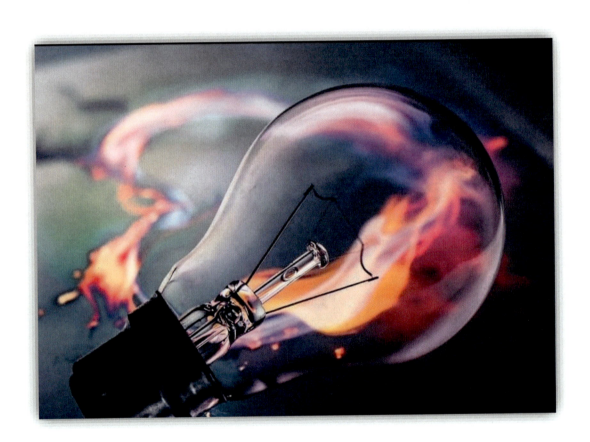

Dear self,

_____

_____

_____

_____

_____

_____

_____

_____

_____

_____

_____

_____

_____

_____

_____

_____

_____

_____

_____

_____

_____

_____

If you are struggling with balance, life transitions, stress, coping, mental health or just life in general...please don't hesitate to reach out to a professional. There is so many licensed social workers, mental health therapists, and marriage and family therapists that would love to help you continue your path to self-improvement. Not everyone who sees a therapist is "mentally ill" or has something wrong with them (societal stigma). We all need a little help and support throughout life, including therapists themselves.

I hope you feel proud of yourself and continue your journey of being the best version of you! 😊

Made in the USA
Middletown, DE
18 December 2020